MW01242995

Poems by

Mark Borisyuk Geller

Power of Love

The knower and known

of life are love while love

in the immortal becomes

the projection of birth

being after death although

love is in and for itself to

love and be loved as its

greater beyond our scope

or sum of all knowledge,

for love is made of our

heart as spirit our heart

knows that which our

mind   cannot,   by

revolution of love, in

spirit, we feel and know

it.

Lady@

Barny lover make up of

one part a beat of life and

love the heart, over what

the heart, our are the

moons light offer across

my teeth, and eyes, the

stars are the pebbles

apple smiles surrender on

a raspberry color of her

brown eyes and tweeted

or charm of her old

heaven in thine sweet

tender kissed lips where

her temple is mystery

much like lemon, in tea,

do think remember your

heart, like flowers, I loop

your heart, in my red

string, here many nice

lovers, I the nicest bee, to

prove a mighty end, I

love you all the more,

lovely lady queen, I will

always hear you, I love

you and you love me,

morning   sun,   nightly

gown, yellow breaks in

not so distant towns,

remember me, how you

used to be, I thank you in

a dream, in the sky the

purple rose, no doubt her

cherry cheeks, around the

heart her tulips, The

wakeful leaves belong in

summer, the sun recedes

the song, in our dream,

she sparks my love with

singing, the warmth of

curls for orchards, the

breadth of life the morn,

the   splinters   in   her

beauty, oh gosh how love

is dumb, we made the

mead the sweetest honey,

the harsh wind will come,

and to the immortal

hawk, he wills a sweep,

the honey's tooth, so ripe

and hoary, o' cherry, the

fare apple doodle in his

palette.

Boom@

hero art child, each field

recouple wheels, letter

price – touching bye, The

leaves the dole in prate,

jungle drain trees fall

knot,　　　sickness　　　and

diamond sock, about evil

nothing　bad　hat,　brain

survival　to　serve　dog,

dear　jerry　queue　in

Braxton, Dr. weep a snip

for balloon, I am a hero

but we couldn't, we count

pioneer in yellow, cleave

the   wonder   mirrored,

Class the heavy pump in

kin, Kipper jean and

swim bean, tux bear

lollypop for wind, we

created the water lime,

under   the   spray   from

weather tooth rear end the

cool pea,

in tree, face the wall in

gang the boat heart, I do

not know a word ferry,

most of all I care to pay

toll, a wash my path with

under, I want the call to

blame all, my brother

gone in wheat... under the

poster I am short, and

under the gone I am in,

some time as none I rose

to, in reality a zero ply

pundits, people to fin

must I obscure, the truth

may take trashed, I am

scared for falling dogs,

never could I take miss

we, I stink the life my par

bodies, the good angel

doesn't call, all I got is

the nail carpeted, Sun

comes out in ingle wall,

the   quail   in   Israel,

Koranic gun was better

zero   button,   sexual

connection zero roll, I

thought I could bring

sexy, I did spend tie on

time   sexy,   rear   end

myself in bear ere, crunch

the bright bust head, from

Weinstein   left   dearest,

she   doesn't   thing

different, hundred miles

roses Texans, but will the

walk from gain, oh boy

the pen, the cheek, other,

ether, or open width, cure

myself the sheep cere, I

cannot pay the awful cars,

bye the cigar for then,

howl, fear nothing all will

tart   me,   this   course

Carolina   spread,   under

the   mast   remain   bam

bam, I demonstrate now

what   the   waitress,

cleaning the toiler boiled

O, the prim do sand a

bankers, tonight dance

chills to goat, sprain the

angle pant when, grain

the ligament in dins.. take

a   huge   beast   ben   que,

Come   home   cake   sun

hams,   cheese,   pickles,

onions,   of,   drive   coast

yams   in   sin   awe,

sometime   cannot   erase

red, open the door to try

quake, it is clear the stick

with shits, the loath mac

junior white, teaches one

to think crimes, stealing

dimes, not throwing fries,

bored my friends trashed,

we are not bud, and I

cannot say we care of,

after all we let the dogs

out, like sum dumb goy.

HART

*Love gives **hours light,***

To nest thy love, from

love, as you may melt

into thy loves grace, in

gapes, as happens

when the light ends, I

too will listen well,

In the nights wedding

bell,

but the hour does a

careful ride, as thy

vow becomes a recent

hallow weed, and now,

the two of hearts hath

sown, a race to

lightning bud my heart

wilt thy yellow sun a

bed, to wed thy right

leave in your love, I've

found the penny of the

sun in your soul too

many rose, too many

songs.

The Girlfriend Helen

Of my smiles my breath

tender lemon, on a lemon

I can on her eyes, the

eyes   cup   beside   her

temple, Starlit knows my

tips at her smile, A down

your cherry of cup on a

charm, and an as in

sweet-sweet surrender the

apple cup, in a foe a nose

to my your sweet cherish,

in like much love much

sweet open heaven, the

mind a raspberry finger at

my finger, put this heart

on an apple mystery goes,

is love like lemon insane

kisses a sweet lipstick, a

nose to breathe open her

sweet cherry hips, her

apples my smiles at the

hart very breast.

Chocolate

Love is art

Love should always,

Be in your heart.

It hums to the moon,

In dim moon light night

A flower as star,

Orion of endless sun,

A Beating of a rose,

And lost in the soul.

Captain America

The night, I am is, then,

for she knows that love is

care, and it is felt in the

loops of thy tears, and no

brown penny could ever,

take you away, when we

feel, that all people care,

in the real, and time

repair, and other things,

can have your dream of

harmony, but smaller

still, than this pebble is,

are certain voices in your

sleep, for they too have

right to sing, and cherry

birds and gentle springs,

you   could   belong,   to

sprout a hart, carry love

to you in spin and laugh,

bare the same respect to

people then, certainly less

fair their wept, smaller is

the pebble then from sea

to shining sea, show me

then the dagger when up

there you will make the

earth feel me.

FRIENDSHIP

In each pebble, hart, in

each pebble, soul. Bee

carried you too, but who

carried Bee, two though,

to   thought,   sum   only

moon, asps, how beauty

is the sun to thought to

thought in through and

through in and for itself.

Made in the USA
Middletown, DE
22 August 2022

71317909R00046